THE FAMILY

IN

THE CAR

A REVELATION

THE FAMILY IN THE CAR

A REVELATION

Narrated by:
Antoine Farrar

Written by:
Brenda Farrar-Ejemai

Bookstand Publishing
www.BookstandPublishing.com

Published by
Bookstand Publishing
Gilroy, CA 95020
2191_4

ISBN 978 1-58909-485-7

Printed in the United States of America

The Family In The Car
A Revelation

For

Antoine
Marjorie
Omotola
and
Brenton

Be Sure To Notice When You're Happy!

THE FAMILY IN THE CAR

TABLE OF CONTENTS

Antoine Farrar

Brenda Farrar-Ejemai

THE FAMILY IN THE CAR
A Revelation

RELEVANT AND TIMELY FOR OUR TIME

The Family In The Car,
A Revelation

We were like seeds planted in soil,
Removed from society,
Unseen,
Now we are flowers in full bloom
Brenda Farrar-Ejemai

The Family In The Car
A Revelation

Brenda Farrar-Ejemai

author of Roast Beef and Gravy and Black Tongue and Poetry From The Heart

This 'on-time' documentary is relevant today with the rise in foreclosures in the nation. It gives a new face to homelessness in that it describes a family who was once sheltered and somewhat privileged. Gone are the days that the homeless can only be described as criminals or mentally ill. Homelessness can involve the middle class, as well.

For more information on The Family In the Car go to: www.TheFamilyInTheCar.com
Or write to: Favor Blooms, P.O. Box 765, Columbia, Maryland 21045

View trailer at: http://www.youtube.com/TheFamilyInTheCar

PREFACE

One of the greatest tragedies in life is to get to the end of it, and not having known one's purpose. Purpose is the driving force in our daily pursuits, as well as, long term goals.

Why is purpose so important? Why is it frustrating not knowing? Purpose gives the stamina to stand when things are shaky. It is important to have it during those times. When purpose is not known, one can become desperate during trying times.

I remember wanting to know my purpose and seeking it for many years, and becoming frustrated when I couldn't find what it was. I also remember the relief I felt when I finally discovered it. I don't believe that I will ever again be in a situation where I question my existence. No more will I have to worry that I am living my life frivolously. I now know the reason why I am here.

The Family In The Car, A Revelation outlines some of the pressures that propelled me to realize my purpose. It was written to reveal a traumatic event that took place over seventeen years ago. An event strategically manifested to not only help others, but myself, as well.

This book was written to encourage, inspire, and give hope to those who are discouraged, uninspired, and hopeless. My trust is that it will give light to your darkness and peace to your storm.

Remember, hind sight always gives a better view of a situation; and the relevancy and timing of this documentary/book is proof of that.

Grace and Peace
Brenda Farrar-Ejemai

INTRODUCTION

We moved back north after living in the south for six months. We didn't have a large family and the family we had wasn't able or willing to take us in. Moving back brought more stress than we had ever imagined.

My mother did everything she could to keep us together.

We ended up living with several families before we found ourselves

IN THE CAR.

THE FAMILY IN THE CAR
A REVELATION

Chapter 1
FROM NORTH TO SOUTH

Our move from New York City to Richmond, Virginia was prompted by my family having to move from my grandmother's house to an apartment in Crown Heights, Brooklyn,

You see, my grandmother married an old friend she knew many years ago. My grandfather had died some years before when I was only a toddler. Soon after, my grandmother relocated to Florida with her new husband. My grandmother had been living at her new husband's apartment. Before moving to Florida, she sold the house to my aunt, my mother's sister, and her husband. My mother lived in that house 17 years.

The same day that my grandmother moved to Florida, my three siblings, my mom and I moved into the apartment that she had been living with her now new husband. My mother never experienced apartment living up until that time. She only lived in a private home; however, the rent was affordable and we had no choice.

After a little over a year living in that apartment, the landlord wanted to raise the rent. We already planned to move, so we continued with our daily routine. One day when we returned home from work and school, we found a sheriff's note on the door and the locks were changed.

Nervous and trembling and not knowing what to do, my mom proceeded back down the winding marble stairs of the six story building. Waiting for the elevator would have taken too long. After walking down those six flights of stairs, we made our way to the corner, where there was a public telephone. My mother called my aunt to ask if we could stay there until our move south. We were planning to move to Richmond, Virginia in two weeks. We were allowed to stay.

Before moving we placed our belongings in storage.

Within two weeks, we were on Interstate 95 South heading to Virginia in our hatchback automobile.

On the way down there, as if we weren't nervous enough already, all of a sudden that steering wheel began to shake uncontrollably. We pulled over to see what was wrong. First we thought it were bumps in the road that were causing the steering wheel to shake. But when it continued to shake, for what we thought was an unusually long time, we knew it had to be something else. After pulling over into a rest stop, we saw that we had a flat tire. We didn't know how to change a tire, so we were relieved when two southern gentlemen offered to change the tire for us. My mother and I both learned how to change a tire after that incident.

Just to let you know how little my mother knew about tires, my mother dumped the entire tire. She threw away the tire and the rim. She did not know she was to save the rim for the new tire. We ended up having to buy a new rim, as well as, a new tire.

We arrived safely in Virginia.

When we saw the apartment we were a little disappointed. It was arranged for us to move there, so we hadn't seen it before the move. I guess if my mom had a choice, that one wouldn't have been it. However, we had gone through so much to get there, we made ourselves comfortable enough to settle in.

My mother found it difficult finding steady work. It was especially difficult to find work that paid enough money to sustain a family of five. At first she worked for temporary agencies and then worked as a security guard part-time at nights. She had no experience as a security guard, but needed a job, any job at that point.

This was a trying time for her, because she had a number of years of experiences as an administrative assistant in major corporations in New York City. She couldn't understand why it was so tough for her to get a good paying job at a prominent corporation or any business. She did, however, understand that the practices of the North were different than the practices of the South in many ways. But this was 1989!

Because we did not have the money to keep up the payments at the storage facility, we lost all of our possessions that were in storage back home in New York. The entire room was auctioned off. Can you imagine? Everything of value was gone. Things that my mom collected during her lifetime were gone. Pictures, albums of pictures, graduation albums, books of all kinds, and sentimental items, things that could never be replaced were gone forever. Some of the items were priceless; because we could never replace them. Those items were the hardest to forget about. We didn't mind losing the other items, as much, because we could buy them again, at some point in the future. My mother was an avid knitter and all of her needles and other supplies for knitting and crocheting were gone.

My mother called the storage company to ask if she could get her personal items, but was told it was too late.

This was an event that we had to put in the back of our minds, if we were to survive and retain our sanity.

Because my mother couldn't find work, after six months living in the south, we made the decision to relocate back to New York City.

My mother was confused as to what to do. She even contemplated giving us temporarily to foster care, until she could get back to New York City and make a way for us. The thought of it was literally heart breaking for her. She was thankful that she didn't have to go that route after all.

Chapter 2

FROM SOUTH TO NORTH

We moved back to New York City in January of 1990. Arrangements were made for us to stay with a lady of a former church we attended. (Being careful not to mention any names)

I'm sure that many of you know that living with people can be one of the most uncomfortable situations you can find yourself in. You have to conform to their rules, and ways. You are actually at their mercy. You are at the mercies of their attitudes and mood swings. You truly never know a person until you have lived with them.

Our experience was no different. There were a lot of disagreements. It had gotten to the point, where the locks were changed on the door so that we couldn't get back in. So there we were again locked out.

Due to the fact that this was a housing project, my mother had to get the housing police to solve the matter. They accompanied her inside so that she could get our belongings from the apartment.

She said it was embarrassing and belittling. It was humiliating for her who, all of her life, led a sheltered life and lived in a private home. She felt like a common criminal having to go the police to seek help as if she was breaking into someone's place.

After being escorted by the housing police, we entered the apartment and retrieved our items. We moved just a half a block away. This time our belongings were in a shopping cart. We pushed everything we owned in a shopping cart to our new location. We were now at my aunt's friend's apartment. Needless to say, it was a short stay.

Chapter 3

A SHELTER IN THE TIME OF STORM

The Search

After suffering through the humiliation of living at these two locations, we were now living in the car. We had very little family and had exhausted all other alternatives. We had nowhere else to turn.

It was the summer of 1989. The summer heat worked to our advantage because we didn't have to worry about the cold winter weather.

That night we drove around Brooklyn, New York looking for a special place to spend the night. By special, I mean we looked for spots in decent neighborhoods where we felt it would be as safe as possible to close our eyes and sleep. This was to be our bedroom, while the car was our shelter from the elements.

Places with bushes and trees were welcome spots because we could hide from being seen. After all, we were sleeping outside on the streets of New York City, and we had to be careful!

After we found the spot for the night, we made our beds.

Chapter 4
THE FAMILY

There were five of us; my two sisters, my brother, and my mom. I was 14 and the oldest. My two sisters were Marjorie then 12 and my younger sister Omotola then 4. My brother Brenton, the youngest, was 2.

At this time in our lives we were a tight knit family. After all that we had gone through to this point, we knew we were all we had. I believe we became more protective of each other than ever before.

Chapter 5
MAKING OUR BEDS

Brenton's bed was made by pulling down one of the folding split seats in the back of our 1983 hatchback. We would spread out a blanket back there, lay him on top of it and cover him up with another. I slept in the front passenger seat, which was a reclining seat. Marjorie and Omotola slept in the one seat left in the back. My mother was in the driver's seat. She could drive away quickly if needed.

You can imagine how cramped it was sleeping in the same position all night with hardly any room to move. We didn't have the room to turn over like we would have been able to do if we were sleeping in a bed. And when morning came, we weren't able to stretch our arms and legs to the fullest, but rather we just repositioned ourselves in our seats, straighten up the best we could, and drove off.

We kept our windows cracked because the windows would fog up while we were sleeping and also we didn't want to keep the air conditioner running all night. The windows fogging up wasn't a good thing because we needed to see everything that was going on outside around us in order to be safe.

It was a scary feeling sleeping outside in the elements, exposed and vulnerable. We knew we were taking chances.

Chapter 6
OUR DAILY ROUTINE

In the mornings we looked for places to wash up. We looked for fast-food restaurants that provided bathrooms for its customers, such as McDonalds. The restrooms were not always clean, but we had no other choice but to use them.

We took turns using the restrooms. My mom went in first with the Omotola and Brenton, while Marjorie and I stayed in the car and waited. When they came out, then we would go in.

When we washed we tried not to touch our wash cloths on any part of the sink. My mother always put paper towels on the floors of the restrooms. We changed our clothes and made sure no part of our clean clothes touched the filthy floors or walls. When we were washing in the bathrooms, we hoped no one was waiting to use them.

We always wondered if people could tell what we were doing in the bathrooms. It took longer to wash up than it did to just use the restroom.

The experience was not only unhealthy, it was humiliating. Having to use public restrooms to wash was degrading for sure.

Chapter 7
KINGS PLAZA

We usually spent our days at Kings Plaza, a mall in Brooklyn. It was our home during the day. My mother would buy food and share with all of us. She tried to stretch whatever money we had. At this time she wasn't working yet, but was waiting to start working at Brookdale Hospital, located near Canarsie in Brooklyn.

All day we would sit on benches in the mall watching people as they went in and out of stores. We did this to past the time away. Many looked happy as they left with their packages and boxes. Life was going on as usual for them, but for us, life had come to a halt. We were just going through the motions of surviving everyday. We weren't doing anything productive, we just existed.

My mother wondered if the people we saw shopping and walking through the mall, had any idea of what we were going through. She also wondered if they could see the distress in our faces. Could they see that we were different? Did they know that when the day was over, that we had nowhere to go? Could they tell that when they left the mall and went home, to snuggle in their beds that we had to go search for ours. Did we show it in our expressions? Could they see our hearts aching? Or did we just blend in with everyone else, and was invisible?

We stayed there from early in the morning, until late at night. We stayed at the mall until the stores were about to close and then went on our search for a place to sleep.

Chapter 8
LONELY NIGHTS

As the sun went down, our search for a place to sleep would start all over again. We wanted to vary the places we slept because we didn't want to be noticed.

However, before we went to sleep, we had to have our dinner, just like most people usually do, before going to bed for the night. We usually had Chinese Food. It was the most reasonably priced fast food that could be shared amongst all of us. We usually bought fried rice and chicken wings and it was quite filling.

Because we didn't have a traditional dining room to eat our meals, we drove and parked in areas where we felt was quiet and away from crowds. We ate in the car and then relaxed there for a little while, just watching people and cars go by.

After awhile, we drove around to search again for a safe place to sleep.

After we found our spot for the night, we would try to get into a good (comfortable) sleeping position. We never parked in the middle of a block because that is where the entrances of houses were. We did not want people who were coming in and out of their homes to see us sleeping in the car. We always chose the street corners which usually had high-fenced garages that would shield us from view. Once we were snuggled in, we would talk. We talked about things just like ordinary families probably did before they fell asleep.

My mother tried to encourage us with her words. She would tell us that things were going to get better soon. I think she wanted to encourage us, so we wouldn't worry about what was going on. She wanted to give us hope that things would get better soon. She was more concerned about our feelings than she was about her own. We were all we had in the world.

Sometimes while struggling to fall asleep, my mother would see people going into their homes and closing the doors behind them. We could see them inside their houses sitting down eating, or lounging on a sofa.

We felt sad and isolated from the world. We cried many times because we had fallen and we wondered how long we would remain there.

Not knowing how long this was going to last, was frustrating. In some cases no news is good news, but it wasn't good news in this situation. Having an idea of when all of this trauma would end, would have eased the anxiety a little.

Chapter 9
SHELTERED AND PRIVILEGED

According to my mom she had a sheltered childhood. Her parents provided them (my mom, her two sisters and her brother) with the education to become important American citizens. They never wanted for anything. There always was abundance.

Her parents owned a three-story house in Brooklyn, New York. There was plenty of food; clothing and even trips were taken, sometimes twice a year. My mother's father was a chef, and his meals were always tasty. She was a chubby adolescent. She used to ask for seconds at mealtimes, and they would scrape the bottom of the pot to get what they called the pot cake. That was the tastiest part. They made home-made ice cream, using an old fashioned ice cream churner. Everyone took turns turning the rock salt, condensed milk and ice. It was hard turning it, but it was good eating it. It was the most delicious tasting; creamy ice cream.

All the children attended notable music schools and became musicians. My mother took piano lessons at a young age at the New York School of Music in Manhattan, N.Y. She learned to play the clarinet in her music classes in Junior High School and High School. All of her siblings were musicians also. Her oldest sister played the bass violin and her youngest sister played the accordion. Her brother learned to play the violin with a private tutor who came to their home to give him lessons.

My mother, and her brother and sisters were all exposed to many social events such as: operas, theater openings, ballet recitals and concerts of the New York Philharmonic at Lincoln Center. My mom told us of a time when she performed at the well-known Carnegie Hall, a famous music hall in New York City. She told me of a time when she, her brother, and sisters all performed at a nursing home for the elderly.

She could remember how grateful the residents of the nursing home were toward them. They were very happy to have them entertain them. My mother also played the clarinet in a Columbus Day Parade with her band from Halsey Junior High School, located in Brooklyn, New York. She was also a member of the New York City All-Boro Band and produced a record album.

My mother never imagined that she would be going through anything this traumatic in her lifetime. How could someone who led a sheltered life, see homelessness in their future? It is unimaginable. She would have told you to your face you were telling a lie, if you had told her she would be going through this.

But she was.

Chapter 10

THE PLEAD

Sometimes my mother would cry and pray in a very low voice, so no one would hear her. Her prayers were like pleads. She prayed to God that He would some how grant us a miracle that would end this ordeal. It was as though if she didn't get a miracle soon, she wouldn't last.

This was usually at the end of the day, during the night, when everyone was tucked in. It was the time when the hustling and bustling had quiet down, and all that was left was time to reflect. It was the time to wonder about how long the situation would last. When would it all come to an end and return to normal again. Hoping that we would awaken from a long sleep and discover it wasn't real at all, but that it was just a nightmare from too much to eat the night before.

We wanted to find everything blissful and wonderful; like it never happened.

Chapter 11
ETHEL CUMMINGS

After several nights sleeping in our car on the street corners, we got tired of the uncomfortable, inhumane, humiliating existence and decided to enter the shelter system. We knew we couldn't possibly continue this type of existence. We also didn't want to be caught.

Before entering, what we call the system, we were offered to have a home-cooked meal and a bath by a loving church mother named Ethel Cummings. Sister Cummings was my mother's second mother for many years. She not only gave us a home-cooked meal and bath, but she also gave us money to have our belongings stored.

After leaving her house, we drove our car to the safest place we could find near the Rockaway Parkway subway station on the L line in Brooklyn. We parked the car and prayed for the safety of our things stored in there, as well as the safety of the car itself. We then proceeded on our way to the Emergency Assistant Unit.

Chapter 12
THE L TRAIN

The train ride on the L train into downtown Brooklyn, New York was a long one. Just knowing where we were on our way to, made it seem longer than usual. It was like knowing you had to go somewhere but not really in a hurry to get there. Dwelling on the horror stories of the shelters caused our stomachs to knot with pain. If we could have thought of another way out, we would have taken it.

Have you ever looked at people and wished that you were them instead of you? Or wished you had their life instead of yours? That is the way we looked at people, we wanted to be them. As if we knew for sure that their life was so much better than ours. We knew nothing about what their life was. But we assumed that they couldn't possibly be going through what we were going through. For all we knew, they might have had situations much worse than ours. But we were willing and eager to be anyone else but us!

You say to yourself 'life isn't fair,' and why is this happening to me. You want to know from God what you did to deserve this punishment. While looking across at people, you're wondering why they have a better life than you do. You ask yourself, what did you do in life that was worse than what they did? You ask that because you knew they had to have done something sinful, everyone has. No one is blameless. Being homeless had to be a punishment for something we had done.

These are not just rhetorical questions either, you really want answers. You want answers because you feel if you get an answer, some how you can understand it all and that would make things more bearable. We cannot say for sure, because we never got an answer as to why. We just believed that it would pass, and that there was a purpose in it. That was our hope. When you have nothing else to hope in, that is what you do, if you are to survive.

Faith is the substance of things hoped for, the evidence of things not seen. We were walking by faith.

INSIDE A NEW YORK CITY TRAIN

Chapter 13

WHEN YOU CAN'T FIND YOUR WAY OUT, YOU'RE TRAPPED

My mother told me that she now knows why a caged animal attacks. He attacks because he's trapped with no way out. When he looks around at his surroundings, all he sees are bars and gates. He wants to be given the opportunity to choose where he goes and comes. That's the way life was intended for him. As long as the animal doesn't complain about his plight, he is considered a good animal. But as soon as he begins to growl and complain, the zoo keeper thinks he is no longer friendly and that he has gone mad. The keeper then puts up a sign that says 'Beware Of Attack Animal'. You would attack too if you were caged and had to watch others peering at you as they walked around freely and uninhibited. Yes, of course, that animal is Mad!

No one wants to feel trapped. No living thing was born caged. Every living thing was born free.

> Born free, as free as the wind blows
> As free as the grass grows
> Born free to follow your heart
>
> Stay free, where no walls divide you
> You're free as the roaring tide
> So there's no need to hide
>
> Born free, and life is worth living
> But only worth living
> 'cause you're born free
>
> Andy Williams
> Words by Don Black

Is not that the truth? These lyrics support the fact that every human being is supposed to be free with no divisions. No walls should divide one from another. However, there are walls that cause division in this society. Aren't there? And, those walls don't seem to be coming down anytime soon. Life truly is only worth living if you are free.

Chapter 14
THE EMERGENCY ASSISTANT UNIT (EAU)

As we entered the EAU we walked into a room with pale walls and plastic seats already filled others seeking shelter. We waited well into the night to be called for a 'van ride' to a shelter sight. The 'van ride' took a group of people to drop off at different shelters throughout the city.

After waiting for many hours that night, we were finally offered peanut butter sandwiches to eat. They were thickly spread with peanut butter on thick slices of bread with hard crusts. The peanut butter was so thick that it stuck to the top of our mouths. We were given some liquid to drink; I believe it was milk, to wash down the 'stick to the roof of your mouth' peanut butter sandwiches.

During the long and tedious wait, my mother was summoned several times up to the window where a city worker was behind a glass.

The longer you have to sit and wait, the more time your mind has to think of all the negative and terrifying events you were destined to face. Summoned is an appropriate word to use because we were literally in the trial of our lives. We knew we had a long road ahead of us.

The city workers were the judges; and we were the defendants. We had to defend why we were there and why we needed the aid of the City of New York. They were ready and geared up to ask the same questions that were asked of the individual before us.

We were probed about the legitimacy of our being there. As if this was something we planned and were looking forward to doing our entire lives, and now we had finally arrived. We knew that they were ignorant, because if we had another way we would have taken it rather than being there and standing before them. There wasn't anything pleasant about this ordeal. Who wants to be drilled? They asked questions such as:

Why were we there? How did we get there? What led up to us having to go there?

Was there anyway we could avoid being there? In other words they wanted to know if our case was authentic. They wanted to know whether or not we were just trying to enter the system to be placed in public housing and get something free from the city of New York.

We heard that many people did that sort of thing just to get an apartment in a public housing project. There is a list to get into that type of housing. Being homeless brought you to the top of the lists. Public housing was very much sought after and most people who got into this type of housing were glad to get in. That was the goal of many of the people we spoke to. Some said they intentionally entered the system just to get on the top of the list of public housing.

That definitely was not the intent of my mother. If anything, she wanted to avoid it. She grew up in a private home all of her life, and this was not something she was after. She was in a predicament that landed her among many who thought this way. But she had higher aspirations.

The whole process was a nightmare to my mother. It was unbelievable. She couldn't believe she was sitting there going through this torment. It was not because she felt she was better than anyone else, but that she wasn't used to that type of humiliation.

You can imagine that sometimes the people, who worked in this type of agency, were not always the nicest. The EAU workers could sometimes be obnoxious and harsh. They seem to try hard to embarrass and degrade people in need. It appeared to be a tactic used to discourage people so that they would give up and go somewhere else.

They acted like the money or the services were coming out of their pockets. We never could understand that. There was barely any sympathy or compassion.

Chapter 15
PRIDE PUT ASIDE

During the long wait at the EAU, my mother decided to make a few phone calls. She thought about all the people she knew. She thought of all the people she knew, as well as, all the people her mother knew. She was sure she could convince someone to take us in, even if it was for a short time.

My mother was always an ambitious and independent person. Therefore she had no doubt that she could pull us out of this situation, if given the opportunity and time to do so.

After making a number of calls to everyone she could think of, she gave in, sat down, and waited to be called to be delivered to some location within the system. She threw in the towel and gave up the fight.

Chapter 16
MEDICAL HISTORIES

We were seen by a nurse who took our medical histories. I suppose this information was needed to know to determine if we had some type of contagious diseases. As we were waiting we saw people being called to go on 'van rides' to be dropped off at shelters throughout the City.

People were placed according to family status. By family status I mean whether or not they had young children. Families with young children or babies six months or under were placed in tier 2 shelters. Others were placed in tier 1 shelters.

The difference between tier 1 and tier 2 shelters was that the tier 2 shelters offered private rooms.

These types of shelters offered protection for young children from infectious diseases such as measles which may be prevalent in open dormitory style shelters known as tier 1's.

A shelter could be a rehabilitated abandoned building, hospital or hotel. Most of the locations we saw, however, were in undesirable locations throughout the city. Many of them were infested with roaches and mice.

Chapter 17
THE VAN RIDE

After hours of waiting we were finally called for the 'van ride'. Our stomachs began to ache. We had no idea what we were going to or where we were going. That ride brought a lot of anxiety. We arrived at a dormitory style shelter in the Bronx, New York.

It was summer, so there were a lot people outside, hanging out. We went in got registered, was seen by a nurse and social worker, and was given blankets and sheets. We were then ushered into a large room with other families, including men, women and children. We received our cots and settled in.

Chapter 18
LIFE AT THE TIER 1

Meals at the tier 1 were served lunchroom style. Families were called down to eat by a bull horn, or word of mouth. Trays were given with pre-packaged meals and families sat on school-type long tables and ate their three meals. Everyone ate together like 'one big happy family'. After awhile you just got used to it. After the meals were finished families returned to their bed areas.

We were fortunate because we had a portable television that kept us entertained while at the sight.

On weekends we weren't there much. We would take the train ride back to Brooklyn, where we parked our car the night before. Our clean clothes were inside the back of the hatchback. We would go the laundromat and wash and fold our clothes and just take with us the amount of clothes we needed for one or two nights. The others were left in the car.

There were times, before my mother began to work again, that we didn't have the fare to pay for the subway rides into the Bronx. So we would walk through the bus depot which led right into the station platform, where the trains waited for passengers to board. The route of the L train ran from Rockaway Parkway in Brooklyn to 8th Avenue in Manhattan. We boarded at the beginning of the line.

Chapter 19
SECRETLY HOMELESS

Everyday early in the morning, while the other people in our dorm were still sleeping, we were up washing and putting on our clothes to take the train ride into Brooklyn where my mother worked and where we went to school.

If you didn't know our situation, you would never have guessed that we were living in a shelter. With the large crowds of people riding the New York City subway system, no one had a clue that we had just left a shelter and would return to it at the end of the day. None of the co-workers, at my mother's job, ever knew she was homeless. She came, did her work, left, and returned each day.

We didn't look like the 'average' homeless person. I mean the ones that are shown in pictures, newspapers and magazines. We weren't lying on the sidewalk with a cup in our hands. We were clean, our clothes were ironed, and we were well dressed.

We also did many of the things other families did. We went to school during the week. On weekends we went shopping, visited friends, family, and occasionally went to see a movie. On Sundays we went to church; and during the week we attended church events.

Even though we didn't have the look of homelessness, we did have the feeling. We had the feeling of hopelessness.

We didn't stop living. However, it felt as though we stopped existing. Inside, we knew we were lacking one of the basic human needs. We existed because we were still alive. Albeit, we didn't give up because of our circumstances; we kept going in faith. We knew somehow that 'this too would pass'.

We were the homeless and the privileged at the same time, if there is such a thing. We were the working class homeless, so that gave us an advantage over others who were homeless and on public assistance. We didn't lack money and we weren't hesitant to give to people who didn't have it.

In reality, we were secretly homeless.

Chapter 20
WITHOUT A VISION THE PEOPLE WILL PERISH

The predicament of some of the homeless seen on the street in living in card board boxes, under bridges and in subway tunnels, is that they have given into their circumstances. They didn't have the fight within them to fight through. Maybe they didn't get the encouragement they needed from friends or family to help them push their way out. Perhaps they just got weary and didn't have the strength to press on any further. Or it might be that time, after time, after time, they were dealt a bad hand and they came to the conclusion that whatever will be will be.

When I was just a little girl
I asked my mother, what will I be
Will I be pretty, will I be rich
Here's what she said to me.
Que Sera, Sera
Whatever will be, will be
The future's not ours, to see
Que Sera, Sera
What will be, will be.

My mother remembers singing that song as a little girl. The lyrics of the song left the impression on her that life simply was up to chance. In other words she felt that she had no control over what happened to her in life. She was just to live and tackle whatever came her way. That is the power of persuasive words.

Que sera sera, whatever will be will be, the future is not ours to see, que sera sera. Of course no one can see the future. That's a good thing. One reason why it is good is that some people wouldn't be able to take it if they could see every traumatic thing that was to come. The picture would be too fear-provoking.

And how is it that some people's 'whatever will be' turned out better than other people's. Who knows the answer to that question?

How much can a person's heart endure with disappointment after disappointment, let down after let down? No one knows the limit.

Picture hanging off a cliff with a short rope. You wish the rope was a little longer so that you can inch your way down to the point where you could at least land safe and sound if you had to jump.

In the same way, they were given the short end of the rope, and when they came to the end of their ropes, no extension was given to them. When they could no longer hold on, they fell off.

The blows of life were knocking them down and the last knock-out was too powerful a punch for them to recover from it. So they stayed down for the count rather than get back up and receive more blows.

Playing it safe was an alternative. Staying out of the game of life kept them out of harms way. If they weren't in game they didn't have to worry about being let down. Only those who were still fighting in the ring had the chance of being knocked down.

HOMELESS MAN DIGGING IN GARBAGE

These people were, most likely, at one time filled with promise. They were filled with the promise that they could succeed in this democracy, if they tried, tried and never gave up. After all, this is the land of the free and the home of the brave. They tried to be brave, but the motivation wore out.

At some time or another in their lives, their vision of hope dimmed. The light at the end of their tunnel became the size of a pin hole, until there was no longer a vision to hold onto. Not able to see their way out of the darkness, they became immobile. Maybe they yearned for a flicker of light, but didn't know where or how to find it.

Chapter 21
SHELTER LIFE

It was summer time, so my sister and I worked for the Summer Youth Employment Program and my younger brother and sister went to day care.

We were not around most of the day to experience the full-spectrum of being homeless. Every weekend we went to our car which was parked in Brooklyn. We usually visited with family and friends or went window shopping.

On occasion we would take a ride out to Coney Island to enjoy the ocean, and food. We loved to watch as people went up and down on the Cyclone, screaming and hollering for their lives. We already new the affects that ride had on the body. Going up was okay, but coming down was sickening. It felt as if your internal organs came up and out of your mouth. And we never could understand why people would hold both of their hands up in the air when the ride was making a descent.

When we rode The Cyclone, we always held on so tight to the bar in front of us, that if it flew off, we would go airborne with it while still holding on. The bar was our security.

So, we remained on the ground and watched the unsuspecting riders eagerly stand in line to go on.

Enjoying outings like this, made our experience a little less stressful and less dramatic because we had something to keep us busy, as well as monetary means to do the things we wanted to do.

The only thing we had to be mindful of was the time. There was a curfew of 10:00 P.M. each night. If the curfew was not met each night, we would have to start all over again at the EAU and be placed somewhere else in the city.

There were times when we would get an overnight pass and be able to stay out pass curfew. That was usually for Thanksgiving, Christmas or New Year's Eve.

I remember getting passes when we lived in the tier II. I was in High School and would had to go on weekend trips with my Outward Bound Class. I never had a problem getting a pass to stay away for the weekend with my school.

My mother was pleased that I was getting out and away on those weekends because it made it feel like I was living a normal life just like any other kid. And none of the students, at school, ever knew that I had a pass to stay out, or where I was living.

We remember times when the L train would pass right over where we lived. The train ran on an outside line and we wondered if anyone we knew was looking at us going in and out of the shelter. Sometimes when the L train would pass by we would bend down on the side of our car and hide.

When we think back at these moments, some of them were really funny. Those were the times we really cherish. And you know we often say we are glad we had them.

At the tier I, females and males slept in the same large dormitory. There were no separate rooms for males and females. Everyone slept together. Husbands and wives with children, single women with children single fathers with children and battered women with children.

Bathrooms had open rows of sinks which were not enclosed for privacy. Everyone brushed their teeth and did whatever they did at the sinks in the open. Mostly they bathed their young children in the sinks; at least that's what my mother did. There were shower stalls to take showers.

At some of the tier 1s there were public bath tubs. By public, I mean that everyone used the same one bath tub. We would always stand up in the tub with our flip flops on and of course in the showers with them on too. We were careful not to touch any sides of the tub or shower walls. We were also careful not to drop our wash cloths on the floor of the tub or show stall.

We managed to keep this up pretty well.

Chapter 22
GUS

I would like to tell the story about Gus. We don't remember Gus's last name, however, we do remember him. We believe he was an angel sent by God. On one particular day, outside the day care that my sister and brother attended, Gus came up to my mother while she was standing by the car. She had not met or seen him before that. I believe he was a rug salesman. Anyway, he began to talk to my mother about his business. He also told my mother that he attended a church called Christian Life Centre. In hindsight, we really believe he came over for another purpose. That purpose was to be a blessing to our family. After talking for a long time, my mother told Gus about our problem.

She doesn't remember all of the entire conversation. However, Gus ended up asking my mother how much she needed. How much she needed? For a stranger to ask her how much she needed at a time like that was overwhelming for her.

We only knew that a sum of money was placed in her hands with no guarantee that it would ever be given back. What kind of person was this? What kind of selfless act was this?

His family was also kind. We can remember one day his wife met us outside with a warm dish of food. We thought this was so thoughtful. On one particular Saturday, we had a flat tire and Gus offered to change the tire for us, and we spent the day together with him and his son in the park.

My mother couldn't wait to receive her first pay check from work so that she could show Gus how grateful she was. On that day she waited for him outside the day care for a long time. She didn't know exactly where he lived and she wasn't going to leave until she saw him. When she finally saw him walking down the street, she started walking toward him. She thanked him over and over again for what he had done.

What a wonderful thing it was to have had the privilege to meet Gus and his family. These were the type of things that soothed us during that time in our lives. There were no words that we could think of to describe that occasion. We believe he was God sent.

Even to this day, it has been very emotional for us to talk about Gus. We hope one day to see him again. God bless Gus and his family wherever they may be.

Chapter 23
MOVING FROM TIER 1 TO TIER 2

We stayed at 2 different tiers, before we were transferred to a tier 2.

This is how we were transferred:

On my first day of school, in September 1989, I had to leave early in the morning, in a dangerous neighborhood, while it was still dark outside. I had to walk about 2 blocks in Manhattan to catch a New York City bus and then take the subway into Brooklyn, just to catch another bus, to school, all alone.

My mother looked out of the barred windows and watched me go down the street until she couldn't see me any longer. I could imagine her stretching her neck until I was out of sight. I left before the rest of the family that morning, because I had to be at school very early that day, it was the first day of school.

I was fourteen years old at the time and I don't think I ever traveled alone before; definitely not on the subways in New York City.

My mother was very protective of us. The sight of me walking down that street in the early darkness of the morning, was too much for her to take.

That same day, she made a phone call and spoke to one of the case workers at our tier I shelter about her problem. By the time we returned home (to the shelter) we saw so many people standing outside, that we thought it was a fire inside or a fire drill. As we walked towards the entrance of the building, the case worker met us with the words "You got the transfer". Those words were like words that someone had just one the lottery. Really, this was a major break through in our lives. We were climbing up the ladder of success, in a low socioeconomic situation. It was the best surprise. We had no idea. We were so happy. What joy we felt. We were told to pack our bags because we were leaving on the ‘van ride’ in the morning.

Not only were we going to a tier II, but we were going to the one of our choice. This shelter was new and within waking distance to my mother’s job. My sister and I had Summer Youth jobs nearby and my younger brother and sister’s day care was also close by.

No longer would we have to get up early in the morning, while everyone was asleep to travel from Manhattan into Brooklyn on the subway and then come back at the end of the day. Now that we were going to Brooklyn, we could drive wherever we had to go. We didn’t have to worry about leaving our clothes in the car in Brooklyn, and hope that the car and everything in it would be safe. We were now going to have our own rooms with a locked door where we could store some of our belongings and not have to leave some of them in the car. This was a great relief for all of us.

We said our goodbyes to the friends we had made, which was very hard do. These people were our extended family since we lived together. However, we could hardly sleep that night, tossing and turning, because of the anxiety of moving on.

Chapter 24
ARRIVING AT FLATLANDS
THE SCARE

When we got to the tier II the next morning, we first sat with a counselor for an intake. It was a three story building, newly built. We were to be on the third floor. My mother liked the fact that we were on the third floor, she hated to live under people who were noisy. An intake consisted of a lot of paper work and answering a lot of questions. At this point we were used to the questions being asked.

Afterward the intake, we were given sheets and blankets and escorted upstairs by a staff member.

When we arrived at our rooms, we heard music playing inside, and our hearts sank because we thought someone was already living there. We didn't want to go back to where we came from.

We were used to setbacks so our minds were conditioned that things would go wrong. Being at Flatlands was like having our own apartment. We had a door that locked and had privacy also. After a moment or two of stomach pains brought on by the fear of having to return to where we just celebrated leaving from, our stomachs became unknotted with relief. The person inside turned out to be the cleaning lady. We breathed a sigh of relief. She was cleaning the rooms for our arrival.

We stayed at the tier II for two years, but not without incident.

Chapter 25
HE WORKED IT OUT!

While living at the Flatlands Shelter, we made quite a few friends. On one particular night, one of my friends decided to play with a B B Gun and he mistakenly shot a B B bullet at a girl who was there with us. I was in his room that he shared with his grandmother.

The girl got hit in her cheeks. Blood started splattering everywhere, on the walls and floor. It didn't stop until we applied a towel to stop it. Within minutes the whole towel was red with blood.

The police and ambulance were called. The police officers came to our rooms asking questions. My mother told them she didn't know anything about it. You can imagine my mother shocked not knowing what was going on. She was scared and angry at the same time.

My mother was the type to stay inside and mind her own business. She didn't mingle and talk to the residents of the shelter very much.

After the investigation, it was found that it wasn't me who had injured the young girl. However, because of my involvement and due to shelter rules, we were in danger of being sent back to a tier 1. We had to come before the Manager, to take an inquisition. This was one of our most trying times, because we were in a predicament that would send us back to the starting point.

My mother was so worried that she could hardly sleep that night. She told me she would beg rather than go back to square one. She made it known to me it was my fault and that I should be the one punished and not the whole family. We were threatened to be transferred because of that incident. My friend and his family had already been transferred to another site because of this incident.

Everything worked in our favor! My mother gave me such a scolding that night (and I'm telling it quite mildly) and she continued to scold me for a long time afterwards. So much to the point that I never did anything foolish like that again!

Chapter 26
SIX MONTHS TURNED INTO TWO YEARS

The normal stay at a tier II was about six months. Our stay turned out to be two years.

We were never around to be called for van rides through the borough to look at apartments. We remember these were weekly runs. We didn't even know there were any van rides taking place until well into our second year there.

We were just going and coming. Everyday we left early in the morning and returned in the afternoon.

We celebrated Thanksgivings, Christmases, birthdays, graduations, and all the events of life. We became more and more comfortable living there. The good part was there were no bills to pay.

There were times when the administration would do room checks. Room checks were done to check rooms for people that shouldn't be there. You see, no visitors were allowed inside the rooms.

So sometimes in the middle of the night we would hear banging on our door because workers wanted to get in to look around.

That was upsetting and embarrassing, to say the least. Here we were in our pajamas and being intruded upon by the people who worked there.

Chapter 27

SEARCHING FOR A PLACE

The time finally came when we were enlisted to go out with the van to search for a permanent place to live. My mother went on a van ride through the borough of Brooklyn. This event was enlightening, as well as, hilarious. It was no surprise to her when they stopped in certain neighborhoods to look at apartments. She always knew when the van was close to homes that were for her to see. They drove through neighborhoods that were clean with beautiful homes. My mom would get excited, but only for short moment, then the let down. But she knew better than that. Just a few blocks further and the whole scenery would change. One of the men on the ride made the comment "we'll be home soon" and everyone burst out laughing.

The apartments that were shown were all renovated, but the neighborhoods were undesirable. They weren't desirable to my mother because she had higher standards.

Due to the fact that we were at the shelter the longest, we had the first choice of apartments. She didn't choose any of the places that were shown during that van run. She gave up her right to first choice to the others who were more than happy to move in. That was my mothers first and last van run.

We stayed there for another year and then we moved.

Chapter 28

BAY VIEW

It is known that people living in shelters have the first choice of living in one of New York City's public housing, which are called projects. So, of course, we had our chance to choose one.

The housing project we were selected to see, was Bay View Projects located in Canarsie in Brooklyn. It was a decent neighborhood to live in, at that time. The Canarsie Pier was about 1/10 of a mile away. We liked going to the Pier to relax. We used to frequent there for picnics and barbeques also. Hence, it wasn't that it was a bad neighborhood, but the apartment was run down. We knew there was something better somewhere out there for us.

One could see that the apartment was painted numerous times because the paint was so thick, the doors couldn't close. It was so thick on the walls; you didn't need a paint scraper to get the paint off. You could peel it off with your bare fingers.

The appliances were dated. I believe green stoves and refrigerators were no longer in style. The floor tiles that were missing were replaced with ones that did not match the rest of them.

Also, the bathroom wasn't cleaned. The manager showing her the apartment told her that all she had to do is use a little 'elbow grease' and the bathroom would look just like new. Wasn't that the job of the maintenance workers? We always thought that apartments were cleaned before the tenants moved in. This was something new. She couldn't believe she was hearing this from him. That was like the worse thing he could have said to her.

Remember, she had never lived in a housing project. Again, it wasn't that she was too good, she just wasn't used to the life style.

After the manager told her she had to clean the bathroom tub that was the last straw. She declined and left out of there in a hurry.

Chapter 29
CHRISTIAN LIFE CENTRE

We met wonderful people. One of them was a security guard named Neil. Neil became a good friend of our family. He was someone we looked up to. We were always glad when he was on duty at Flatlands. He was always friendly and he made us feel more comfortable. Neil was also a member of Christian Life Centre, which was located on Linden Boulevard, only a few blocks away from the shelter. We now knew 2 people who were members of that church, so we decided to visit. We visited the church a few times and became members of that church also.

Being a part of the church brought a sense of belonging to our lives. We started going to a lot of the events there. We attended the Spiritual Growth Class. My mother and I were baptized there, and my younger siblings were christened there. We went to church on Sundays, as well as, on Tuesday nights. Going there made our ordeal less stressful and hope was restored. We loved the ministry of Dr. A. R. Bernard. We were very happy and were now feeling like normalcy was returning to our lives.

Neil held a weekly bible study on Friday nights. Sometimes all of us attended the study. But I attended more than anyone else did. I tried not to miss a Friday. Sometimes it would be only Neil and I at the study.

Eventually, Neil allowed me to run my own bible study with a small group of children. He was confident that I was capable of handling it.

Chapter 30
FAVOR BLOOMS

My mother went back to college to finish her degree while we were at the Tier II. She decided it was the best time to do it because we had the support we needed while in the system. It was a safety net. All she had to do was concentrate on studying and getting good grades.

She involved herself in many activities of college life. She wanted to take advantage of all the things she had missed out on when she was younger. She was a dedicated student. Nothing could deter her.

She attended Medgar Evers College for her undergraduate studies, and then went on to Brooklyn College to pursue a graduate degree. Both of the colleges were located in Brooklyn, New York and part of the City University of New York.

Her experience at Medgar Evers College was one of the best experiences of her life. She believed she would not have had the same rich experience at any other college.

She attended many cultural events, book festivals, and writers' conferences, among many other activities. At the writers conferences she had a chance to mingle with people such as Walter Mosley, Amiri Baraka, Jasmine Guy, and Terry McMillan.

She also had the privilege to meet and know Betty Shabazz, the late wife of Malcolm X. Mrs. Shabazz was a staff member at Medgar Evers College during the time my mother was a student there. My mother told us of a time when she was in the cafeteria with my youngest sister Omotola. Mrs. Shabazz came in and started talking to Tola. My mother told Tola that she was talking to the wife of the late Malcolm X. My mother returned years later to Medgar

Evers College to attend Mrs. Shabazz's memorial service, held at the college.

My mother also had the privilege of meeting Coretta Scott King, the wife of the late Dr. Martin Luther King. Mrs. King was the key speaker at her graduation.

Education was mom's main priority at that time, after us of course. She proved that it was not only doable but obtainable if wanted badly enough. She was on the Dean's List at her college for 4 semesters. She was an honoree of the National Dean's List Award for two consecutive terms. The National Dean's List Award publishes a book annually that recognizes students all over the nation for their exemplary work and for attaining a grade point average of more than 3.50 at universities. My mother's biography is featured in their 1995 edition.

She believed she would not have had the same experience at any other college.

Chapter 31

A PLACE TO CALL HOME

After 2 years of being homeless, we moved into our new home. It was a brand new construction and close to everything we needed.

Sometime before that we joined hands and prayed as a family to get this place because we were scheduled to move to another place which was further away from our schools and my mother's work. So again, the Lord worked everything out in our favor.

We had rid ourselves of the stigma of homelessness.

We no longer had to sign it and out. We didn't have to abide by any more institutional rules. There were no more worries about meeting curfews. We could come and go as we pleased. No more intrusion of privacy, in the form of room checks. No more hiding and dodging from being seen entering and coming out of the shelter.

It took a while getting used to not having to watch the clock. It was a wonderful feeling when we realized we had been set free.

We thought this must be the way people feel when they are let out of prison. We understood that it took a long while to recondition the mind to new rules, or rather no rules.

When you're used to a certain lifestyle, it becomes second nature to you. I'm sure people who have been released from whatever states of captivity were at first confused. They were probably confused about what to do. Before they were freed, they didn't have to think about those things. Those decisions were made for them. They didn't have to make decisions for themselves.

They most likely had to sit down and think about what they should do first. They were free to go anywhere they chose. When they were captive they most likely discussed with someone, or thought about, all the things they were going to do when they were exonerated.

When you're used to being told what to do, when to do it, and how long to do it, it can be difficult to make decisions on your own. For so long, your basic needs were provided for, and there was hardly ever a time when you needed to make a decision for yourself.

You wouldn't understand this unless you've experienced it.

Although we were not behind prison walls, our leaving the system and being 'free' took time to get used. We started planning all types of places we could go visit and we didn't have to ask for a pass to stay out all night. We could now go anywhere visiting and stay after 10:00 p.m. It's like having the choice of anything we wanted from a candy store, and not knowing what to choose first. It was a great feeling!

We had rid ourselves of the stigma of homelessness. What freedom we felt.

My mother graduated two years after we moved into our new home. She graduated with honors.

During her years in school, she developed a love for writing. While studying in the library of her college, she wrote her first poem. The title of the poem was **EXPERIENCE**. For some reason, however, that particular poem was never published.

Some years later, my mother received confirmation that her purpose in life was to write.

Through it all, our experiences led to many friendships. We met people from all walks of life who came from different situations that led them all to the same place.

Although we endured difficult times, we also enjoyed episodes of extreme joy. We developed unforgettable friendships, and met remarkable people. Looking back now we say, thank you for the journey. In hindsight, we know that things do work together for good, because we now know our purpose in life.

WHAT A GIFT!

I am 27 years old now, a college graduate and the CEO of my own business. My youngest sister, Tola, is eighteen and a pre-med student. My brother Brenton, the youngest sibling, graduated with honors from Junior High School. Marjorie is working at a foundation that finds cures for diseases. And my mom, well, she became a writer, an educator, a conference speaker, and an entrepreneur.

Thank you Jingle Bells

We were like seeds planted in soil,
Removed from society,
Unseen,
Now we are flowers in full bloom.
Brenda Farrar-Ejemai

www.TheFamilyInTheCar.com

ABOUT THE AUTHOR

In 1994, Brenda Farrar-Ejemai wrote her first piece of literature, a poem, entitled: 'Experience'. Two years later, in 1996, her children's book: ***Roast Beef and Gravy and Black Tongue*** was written. In 1998, both ***Poetry From The Heart*** and a motivational series (including ***The Goal***, ***Worry***, and ***Fear***) were published. The documentary: ***The Family In The Car, A Revelation***, (written in 2004) is her fourth book.

Ms. Farrar-Ejemai is an educator and conference speaker. She is a contributing editor for BrooWaha Newspaper, located in New York, Los Angeles, London and Paris. She is also a board member and Training Director, of the United Black Writers Association.

She was born and raised in New York City. There she attended elementary, junior/high school, and college. After attending the City University of New York, she graduated Magna Cum Laude, with degrees in education/sociology.

Favor Blooms, LLC was started in 1994 by Brenda Farrar-Ejemai, and was birthed out of the need to produce work that was not only significant, but timely.

ABOUT THE NARRATOR

Antoine Farrar was born in the East New York section of Brooklyn, New York. This area was considered to be one of the worst neighborhoods in the country. He spent most of his childhood in East New York.

Antoine lived in a single-parent household with his mother, two sisters and his brother. Antoine is the eldest. Despite having many challenges, Antoine went on to attend and graduate from Brooklyn College. After several 'successful' years of a career in banking, Antoine was able to retire out of the field.

He now enjoys much success and fulfillment as the CEO of his company.

CREDITS

Pictures – BigStockPhoto.com